THE SHEPHERD'S VOICE:

Basic Bible Truth
Step-by-Step

An Introduction to the Christian Faith
for Inquirers and New Christians

"My sheep hear my voice, and I know them and they follow me." John 10:27

Pastor James P. Balson, Jr.

Table of Contents

Lesson 1

The Bible

1   Various titles are used for the Bible within the Bible itself. Write some of them down as you go through this lesson.

        _____

        _____

        _____

        _____

2   Read II Timothy 3:14-17 and answer the following questions.

What is able to make you wise concerning salvation?

_____

Who inspired the Bible? _____

How much of the Bile is inspired? _____

What is the Bible useful for?

        _____

        _____

        _____

        _____

The Bible is _____ to get you ready for

all good works.

3   How long will the Bible last?

          Psalm 119:89; Isaiah 40:8;
          Matthew 24:35; I Peter 1:24, 25

          _____

4   Why is it a good idea for us to read and learn what the Bible

says?

          Romans 15:4 _____

          Psalm 119:9,11 _____

          John 20:31 _____

5   According to Psalm 119:105 the Bible is like a

      _____

6   How should a person respond to the Bible when he or she

reads or hears it?

          I Thessalonians 2:13 _____

          James 1:22 _____

7   II Peter 3:15,16 says that some things in the Bible are

          _____ to understand.

8   Read I Corinthians 2:12,13. If we want to understand what the

Bible means we must depend on the help of a particular

person - The Holy Spirit. He teaches us to

compare _____ with _____.

9   How does God describe the person who "delights" in the Bible

and "meditates" on it all the time? Psalm 1:1-3

_____

10   HOMEWORK: Memorize II Timothy 3:16

Lesson 2

God

1   Who created heaven and earth? Genesis 1:1

_____

How long did it take? Exodus 20:11 _____

2   Revelation 4:11. Since God created everything, He is

_____ to receive glory and honor and

power. In other words, He ought to be worshiped.

3   What is God like? Next to each verse write the characteristic.

God is ....

Isaiah 6:3 _____

Psalm 90:2 _____

James 1:17 _____

Genesis 17:1 _____

John 4:24 _____

Psalm 139:7-10 _____

Psalm 147:5 _____

Job 42:1,2 _____

Psalm 36:5 _____

I John 4:8-10 _____

Psalm 145:8,9 _____

4   The Bible teaches us that there is only _____ true

God. Isaiah 44:6

The Bible also teaches that there are 3 persons who are

identified as this one God:

Galatians 1:1 God the _____

John 20:28,29 _____

Acts 5:3,4 The _____

The Bible truth regarding God being one AND three at the
same time has been labeled by theologians as the TRINITY.

Note how all three persons are found together in these various verses:

Matthew 3:16,17; Matthew 28:19,20; II Corinthians 13:14; I John 5:7

(Note: Some have claimed that I John 5:7 is not really part of the original Bible but was added by men in AD 400. This is incorrect, as this text is referred to in the writings of early Christians such as Tertullian [AD 215], Cyprian [AD 258], and Priscillian [AD 385].)

5 Psalm 66:7. God _____ by His

   power.

6 Daniel 4:35. Who can stop God from doing what He plans?

   _____

7 Psalm 68:19. God _____ us with benefits (blessings)

8 God never becomes _____ Isaiah 40:28

9 I Samuel 16:7. Men and women see the outward appearance

   but God looks upon _____

10 God hates _____ Proverbs 6:16-19

11 Romans 1:18. God has revealed His _____

   against all ungodliness.

12 Revelation 20:11,12. At the end of time God will

   _____ the dead.

13   What makes the difference between being condemned or

        gaining eternal life? John 3:16-18

14   HOMEWORK: Memorize Revelation 4:11

Lesson 3

Jesus

1   How long has Jesus existed? Micah 5:2

        _____

2   Jesus is called "the Word" in the first chapter of the Gospel of

        John. Note the important facts in John 1:1-3:

        "In the beginning _____ the Word [Jesus was

        already there at the beginning] and the Word was _____

        God [Jesus is a separate person from God the Father] and the

        Word _____ God [Jesus is true God, the

        same as the Father]...._____ things were created

        by Him."

3   One Old Testament title given to Jesus is **Emmanuel**.

        According to Matthew 1:23 what does it mean?

_____

4   John 5:23. Jesus says that He should receive the same

        _____ as the Father.

5   What two titles did Thomas use to address Jesus in John 20:28?

        my _____ & my _____

6   What name does God the Father use in addressing His Son,

        Jesus?   Hebrews 1:8 _____

7   According to Titus 2:13 Jesus is both the great _____

        and our _____.

8   Jesus was born of the _____. Isaiah 7:14

9   Isaiah 9:6. In Bethlehem, a _____ was born (His

        Humanity) and a _____ was given (His Deity).

10   When Jesus was born God was manifest [appeared] in the

        _____.   I Timothy 3:16

11   Why did Jesus come into this world? I Timothy 1:15

        _____

12   Acts. 4:10-12. Only through the name of _____ can

        one be saved [forgiven and reconciled to God]

13   According to Jesus, is there any other way to heaven? John 14:6

14   According to I Peter 2:22 is Jesus trustworthy?

_____

15   What did Jesus do in order to bring us to God? I Peter 3:18

_____

16   Why did Jesus die as a substitute for guilty sinners?

        Romans 5:8; Revelation 1:5

_____

17   Christ died for our _____. He _____ again

        after 3 days. I Corinthians 15:3,4

18   Jesus literally and physically rose from the dead. How do you

        know? Luke 24:36-46

19   Jesus died to save sinners. How can we receive the gift of

        Salvation?

        John 3:16
        John 1:12
        Acts 16:29-31

_____

20   HOMEWORK: Memorize John 3:16

Lesson 4

Sin

1   When God made everything, He made it

_____ Genesis 1:31

Ecclesiastes 7:29. God made man

_____

2   If God didn't create the world with sin, who brought it into

the world? Rom. 5:12

One _____

What else accompanies sin? _____

3   I Corinthians 15:22 . What man is responsible for bringing in

this first sin?

_____

4   What is another name for Adam's sin? Romans 5:19

_____

5   If sin can be defined as disobedience, _who_ or _who_ is being

disobeyed? I John 3:4

6   How many times does one have to disobey God's law in order

to be guilty? James 2:10 _____

7   Read the portion of God's Law called The Ten Commandments

in Exodus 20:3-17.

Jesus, teaching about the Law, explained that the mind and
heart are also involved in obedience (or disobedience). Read
Matthew 5:21,22,27,28..

Ask your self, *"Have I ever disobeyed God's law?"*

8   Clearly, doing wrong is sin. James 4:17 says that it is also

sin when we _____

9   How is sin described in these verses:

Isaiah 53:6 - We have gone _____

and turned to our _____

Romans 3:23 - we have_____ of the glory of God

10   List some of mankind's faculties which are affected by sin.

Genesis 6:5; Jeremiah 17:9; Matthew 15:19

_____

_____

_____

11   God made a promise to Israel, and (through Jesus) to all who

trust in Christ. It's called the New Covenant.

What does God promise to do? Ezekiel 36:26,27

_____

12   Being perfect, Jesus didn't deserve to suffer or die. Yet, He did.

Why? I Peter 2:24; 3:18

_____

13   If the wages of sin is _____ (Romans 6:23), and if

Jesus paid the wages for sinners by dying as a substitute, then

consider the significance of Acts 2:24

14   Proverbs 28:13 - What is the wrong response to our sin?

_____

What is the right response to our sin? _____ &

_____ it.

15   Jeremiah 31:33,34 also talks about the New Covenant. For those

who have trusted in Christ, God makes promises regarding sin

& iniquity. What are they?

God will f_____ & r_____ no more

16   I John 1:8. Will the Christian ever reach sinless perfection in

this life? _____

17   I John 1:9 . What does God promise to the Christian who has

      sinned? _____

18   HOMEWORK: Memorize Romans 3:23

Lesson 5

Salvation

1   What were the good tidings (good news) delivered by the angel

     when Jesus was born?

     Luke 2:10,11_____

2   "Good news" is sometimes translated in the Bible by the word

     "Gospel." According to I Corinthians 15:1-4, what is the

     content of the Gospel message? _____

     _____

3   Where did the Apostle Paul learn the Gospel message?

     Galatians 1:11,12   _____

4   Romans 1:16. The Gospel is the _____ of God, unto

     _____ to _____ who

     _____.

5   II Timothy 3:15. The Scriptures reveal that salvation is through

_____ in _____.

6   How can someone be saved? Romans 10:9-13.

He or she must:

believe with the _____

confess with the _____

believe on _____

call on _____

7   Is there any other way of salvation other than through personal

faith in the Lord Jesus Christ?

Acts 4:12 _____

8   If we can be saved by faith in Christ, what are we saved from?

Romans 5:8,9 _____

9   What is the cause of this wrath? Romans 1:18

_____

10   Describe the BEFORE and the AFTER for salvation
.
Ephesians 2:1-6

BEFORE   **AFTER**

_____   _____

_____   _____

_____   _____

_____   _____

11   Read Ephesians 2:8,9.

For by _____ are ye saved

through _____; and that not of

yourselves: it is the _____ of God: not of

_____, lest any man should boast.

12   Titus 3:5. Our salvation is **not** because of our

_____ of righteousness.

13   HOMEWORK: Memorize Ephesians 2:8,9

14   Are you saved?

Lesson 6

The Holy Spirit

1   Ephesians 1:13. After a person hears the Gospel and believes,

he or she is sealed with the _____ _____ who was

promised. (This refers to the ancient practice of using

hot wax and a personal stamp to show that a document was

genuine, finished, and secure.)

2   John 14:26; 15:26. Who promised to send the Holy Spirit to the

disciples? _____

3   When the Holy Spirit comes into a persons life, how long does

He stay? John 14:16 _____

4   Can the "world" (the non-christian) receive the Holy Spirit?

John 14:17 _____

5   Romans 8:9 Every single true Christian has the Holy

Spirit. Those that don't have the Spirit are not _____.

6   Acts 5 tells the account of a husband and wife who agreed

together to lie about how much money they were giving to the

Lord. According to Acts 5:3, they lied to

_____. In so doing, they were, in fact,

lying to _____ Acts 5:4.

7   Read Jeremiah 31:33,34.

Who is speaking? _____

According to Hebrews 10:15-17, which quotes from the book of

Jeremiah, who said those words? _____

8   Titus 3:3-5 speaks of the special work of the Holy Spirit at the

minute of conversion. It's called the washing of

_____ and _____ of the Holy Ghost.

9 The Holy Spirit baptizes (immerses) the new Christian into

_____ I Corinthians 12:13

10 Whose body? I Corinthians 12:12 _____

Ephesians 1:20-23. Another name for this body is the

_____

11 List some of the activities of the Spirit in the life of the

Christian:

Romans 8:26 _____

Acts 1:8 _____

Romans 8:15,16 _____

John 14:26 _____

II Corinthians 3:18 _____

I Corinthians 12:1,8-10 _____

12 Some of the gifts mentioned were temporary because they had

a unique purpose. In the days before the completion of the

Bible, they served to authenticate the message being spoken.

List some of these unique "authenticators" Hebrews 2:4

s_____, w_____ and m_____

13   I Corinthians 13:8 tells that some gifts will end. Which ones?

      _____

14   We already observed that we should not lie to the Holy Spirit.

      What else should we be careful to avoid in our relationship to

      Him?

      Ephesians 4:30 _____

      I Thessalonians 5:19 _____

12   Ephesians 5:18. The Christian should be _____ with

      the Spirit. In the same way the drunk's controlling influence is

      wine (it affects all he says and does) even so, the

      Christian's controlling influence, **affecting all his decisions**

      and reactions is the _____

13   HOMEWORK: Memorize John 14:16

Lesson 7

The Christian Life

1   When a person becomes a Christian he or she become a

_____ II Cor. 5:17

2   The new Christian becomes a part of a new

       _____ Colossians 1:13

       and a member of a new _____Ephesians 2:19

3   I Peter 2:2. If the new Christian is to mature and grow, he needs

       to feed on the _____ in the same way that a baby

       feeds on milk.

4   By spending time in the Word the Christian's mind will be

       _____ and he or she will learn the

       _____ of God. Romans 12:2

5   Luke 18:1. The disciple of Jesus needs to pray

       _____

6   I Timothy 2:1-3. The disciple of Jesus needs to pray for

       _____

7   Philippians 4:6. The disciple of Jesus needs to pray about

       _____

8   Hebrews 10:24,25. The Christian is warned to be careful that he

       does not _____

9   Matthew 5:13-16. The Christian life is described as being like

_____ & _____

10 The Christians whole life should be lived for

_____ I Cor. 10:31

11 Romans 12:1. In other words the Christian gives himself to

God as a living _____ which is

_____ and _____ to God.

12 Paul said in Rom. 12:1 that this life dedicated to God is "your

reasonable service."

Why is such a godly life reasonable for the Christian?

_____ I Cor. 6:19,20

13 The old sinful tendencies in the Christian are called the "OLD

MAN." How should the Christian respond to these old sinful

tendencies? _____ Colossians 3:8,9

14 In other words, the Christian shouldn't give in and let sin

_____ Rom. 6:12

15 What promise does God give in regards to temptations the

Christian might face?

I Cor. 10:13_____

16 What should a Christian do if he or she does sin? I John 1:9

17   The child of God must guard both his actions as well as his

_____ II Corinthians 10:5

What kinds of things should the Christian let his mind dwell

on? Philippians 4:8_____

18   II Timothy 3:12. The godly Christian shouldn't be surprised if

he faces _____

19   Philippians 4:4. What emotion should characterize the

Christian? _____

20   HOMEWORK: Memorize Psalm 1:1,2

Lesson 8

Baptism and The Lord's Supper

1   In the "Great Commission" Jesus left ongoing instructions for
his disciples through all time. Note the sequence of events that
He announced for Christians – Matthew 28:19,20

First - "Teach" - In the original Greek, this word means "*to make
one a disciple*"

Second - Those who become disciples are to be
b_____

Third - Finally, these baptized disciples are to spend their Christian lives learning ("Teaching" in verse 20 is a translation of a <u>different</u> Greek word - this one means "*to instruct*") and doing what Jesus commanded.

2   Who gets baptized in Acts 2:41?

_____

3   What are some of the particular truths of the "word" which

they "gladly received" in Peter's message?

vs. 23,24 _____

vs. 36 _____

vs. 38 _____

vs. 21 _____

4   The people in Acts 8:12 were baptized when they

_____

5   The Ethiopian Eunuch could be baptized only if he

_____with _____Acts 8:36,37

6   Baptism is meant to portray one's personal faith and

identification with the Lord Jesus. In particular, baptism

portrays the _____, burial, and

_____of Jesus. Romans 6:3,4; Colossians 2:12

7   Acts 2:41. After the new Christians were baptized they were

_____ to the local church.

Read I Corinthians 11:23-32 and answer these questions about

The Lord's Supper (also called "Communion"):

8   The bread points to _____ and the cup points to

_____ vs. 23-25

9   What is the purpose in eating the bread and drinking the cup?

vs. 24,25 To _____

10   What is shown by this Lord's Supper? vs. 26

_____

11   When will churches stop celebrating the Lord's Supper? vs. 26

_____

12   As the Christian prepares to partake of the Lord's Supper he

should _____ vs. 28

13   What might happen if someone doesn't examine himself or take

care of sin in his life?

vs. 29-32_____

14   What is the underlying reason why Christians obey these two

commands of Jesus as well as the other things he

commanded? John 14:15 _____

15   HOMEWORK: Memorize John 14:15

Lesson 9

The Church

1   Who owns the church and builds the church? Matthew 16:18

       _____

       Matthew 16:16. It is built upon truth. The truth of

       who_____ is.

2   Jesus purchased the church with

       _____. Acts 20:28

3   How does Jesus feel about the church? Ephesians 5:25

       _____

4   Ephesians 5:23. Jesus is the_____ of

       the church.

5   What is the ultimate purpose of the church?

       Ephesians 3:21_____ .

6   The word "church" is the translation of the Greek word that
    means "a called-out assembly". Thus, in the Bible CHURCH
    always refers to **people**, not a building.

    These gathered people are *like* a

    _____. I Corinthians 3:16

7   I Peter 2:5. They are like a spiritual temple and a spiritual

    priesthood in that when they gather, the people offer

    spiritual _____

8   The members of the church offer the sacrifice of

    _____ Hebrews 13:15

9   They also offer _____ as living

    _____ Romans 12:1

10 Acts 12:5. One important activity for the gathered church

    is _____.

11 The church also gathers in order to be

    _____ . Acts 11:26

12 The members of the church also have responsibilities towards

    each other.

    List a few of them:

    John 13:34,35 _____

Romans 14:19 _____

I Corinthians 12:25 _____

Galatians 5:13 _____

Galatians 6:2 _____

Ephesians 4:32 _____

Ephesians 5:21 _____

Colossians 3:16 _____

I Thessalonians 4:18 _____

Hebrews 10:25 _____

I Peter 4:9 _____

13   I Corinthians 14:26. Everything that is done in the church

should be done unto _____

I Corinthians 14:40.

And be done _____ and in

_____

14   What are the two kinds of leaders God has appointed for his

churches?

Philippians 1:1 _____ and

_____

15   Bishops are also called elders (I Peter 5:1,2)

and _____ Ephesians 4:11 (hint: it's not

apostle, prophet, or evangelist).

In Acts 20:17 & 28 Paul tells the **elders** that they are overseers [lit. "**bishops**"] and that they must feed the flock [lit. "serve as **pastors**"]. These three terms all describe the same men.

16   Deacons were first elected in Acts 6:1-5. Their responsibility is

to take care of the physical concerns of the congregation so

that the spiritual leaders can focus on

_____ and _____ of the

Word. Acts 6:4.

I Tim. 3 records God's requirements for pastors and deacons.

17   HOMEWORK: Memorize Ephesians 5:25

Lesson 10

Assurance of Salvation

1   According to I John 5:13 it is possible to

_____ you have eternal life.

2   When God saves us, it's not because of our works but because

of His _____ and grace. II Timothy 1:9

3   God's purpose is also called His counsel. How much of God's

counsel will He bring to pass? Isaiah 46:10

_____ .

4   John 3:36. When someone believes on Jesus and is saved he or

she _____ eternal life.

5   John 3:18. The Bible teaches that the one who believes on Jesus

is not _____ .

Romans 8:1. There is no _____ to

those who are in Christ Jesus

6   John 10:27-29 tells us that Jesus gives His people

_____ life and they shall

_____ perish and _____ can take

them from His hand or His Father's hand.

7   Will Jesus ever cast away His people? John 6:37

_____

8   In salvation, God begins a good work. How long will God

continue His good work? Philippians 1:6 _____

9   In salvation we commit our souls and eternity into God's

safekeeping. God is _____ to keep safe what we

have committed unto Him. II Timothy 1:12

10 II Timothy 4:16-18. Even though men let him down, the Apostle

Paul's assurance was based on the fact that God was with him

and God would _____ him even unto heaven.

11 Romans 5:8-10. God has already shown the greatest love. He

saved us when we were _____

and _____. Now that we **have been**

justified and being reconciled we **shall be**

_____ from wrath.

12 Romans 8:33,34. Even though Satan might accuse us,

_____ who rose again and

paid the full price for our sins makes intercession for us.

13 Jesus is able to save us to the

_____ Hebrews 7:25

14 When we are saved Jesus gives us the Holy Spirit.

How long will the Holy Spirit dwell with us? John 14:16

_____

15 Ephesians 1:13. After you believe on Jesus, you are

_____ with the Holy Spirit.

16 Ephesians 1:14 . The Holy Spirit is also the

_____ of our eternal inheritance.

E_____ means a *guarantee* or *down-payment*.

17 Hebrews 12:2. Jesus is both the _____ as well as the

_____ of our faith.

The genuine Christian will never lose his salvation for it's entirely God's work, not his own.

18 HOMEWORK: Memorize Romans 8:30,31

Lesson 11

Future Events

1 Isaiah 46:9,10. God declares to us both things that happened in

"ancient times" as well as things

_____ .

2 In John 14:2,3 Jesus promises His disciples that He will

_____ again

and _____ them to Himself so that they

will always be with _____ .

3 I Thessalonians 4:13-18 gives more details about Jesus' return.

When he returns the saints who are _____ will

rise first, then the saints who are _____ will be caught

up to meet Jesus in the air.

4   When Jesus comes back for us, He will change us so that we

will be _____. I John 3:2

5   That change is described in I Corinthians 15:50-53. It is a change

from corruptible to _____ and from mortal to

_____. The change will happen

in a _____.

6   What kind of inheritance does Jesus have waiting for

Christians? I Peter 1:3,4

_____

7   I Thessalonians 5:9. After Jesus takes all the Christians off the
earth there will be time of tribulation when God will send
judgments on the earth. God has been long-suffering a very
long time, but one day His wrath will be revealed (Revelation
6:17). Christians will be in heaven with Jesus during this time
because God has NOT appointed us to

_____

8   Matthew 24:21 . When Jesus described the time of Tribulation

He said it would be a time of _____ Tribulation,

such as this world has _____ known.

9   II Thessalonians 2:3,4. During the years of Great Tribulation a particularly wicked man will arise. He is sometimes called the Anti-Christ.

He will oppose G_____ and exalt h_____.

10   Revelation 16:14-16. The Great Tribulation will come to a conclusion in a battle named for its location,

_____

11   That great battle is described in Revelation 19:11-19. What are some of the names or titles given to the Lord Jesus Christ?

_____

12   Who returns WITH Jesus at this time? Jude 14,15

His _____

13   Romans 14:10-12. The saints will one day stand before the Judgment Seat of Christ.

Each will give _____ of Himself .

14   According to Revelation 20:4, Jesus will rule this earth for

_____ years.

15   A final judgment before the GREAT WHITE THRONE is described in Rev. 20:11-15.

ALL the rest of dead will be judged. B_____ will

be opened. Everyone whose name is not in the B_____

of L_____ will be cast into _____.

16   In II Peter 3:10-13 we are told that God will make

_____.

Christians, understanding these things, should live

_____ lives.

17   In light of these certain future events what should be our

response? Luke 12:40 _____!

18   HOMEWORK: Memorize John 14:2,3

Lesson 12

Witnessing

1   Why did Jesus come to earth? Luke 19:10

_____

2   Jesus had _____ on people because they

were like lost sheep without a shepherd. Matthew 9:36.

3   What is Jesus' prayer request? Matthew 9:37,38

_____

4   In the same way the Father _____ the Son, even

       so, the Son _____ his disciples. John 20:21

5   What was Paul's heart desire and prayer in regards to his

       countrymen? Romans 10:1

       _____

6   Besides praying, Paul also _____ men

       II Cor. 5:11. In order to persuade, Paul

       _____ Acts 18:4.

7   II Corinthians 5:20. Disciples are like

       _____ for

       Christ. Our great desire should be that people be

       _____ to God.

8   Where should the good news (gospel) be preached? Mark 16:15

       _____

9   In Acts 1:8 Jesus tells us that as we go into all the world we will

       be _____ unto him.

10   A witness tells his friends what Jesus did for

       _____ Mark 5:19

11   As we are witnessing in all the world we share a message of

       _____ and _____ of

sins. Luke 24:47 (Remission means forgiveness)

12   Acts 20:20,21. How does Paul summarize his witness

everywhere he went? He testified

_____ towards God and _____

towards the Lord Jesus.

13   If someone is converted when we witness to them, a

_____ is saved. James 5:20

14   If someone is converted, there is _____ in

heaven. Luke 15:10

15   Why should we never be ashamed of the gospel? Romans 1:16

_____

16   Here is a progression of verses that will help you to explain to
      the unbeliever:

Who God is
How God has been wronged (sin)
The just penalty for that sin
God's provision for Salvation through Jesus
The necessity for faith and repentance.

1 Revelation 4:11
2 Romans 3:23
3 Romans 6:23
4 Romans 5 8
5 I Peter 3:18
6 John 14:6
7 I Corinthians 15:3,4

8 Romans 10:9,10
9 John 3:36

17   HOMEWORK: Memorize Romans 1:16

Memory Verses

II Timothy 3:16
Revelation 4:11
John 3:16
Romans 3:23
Ephesians 2:8,9
John 14:16
Psalm 1:1,2
John 14:15
Ephesians 5:25
Romans 8:30,31
John 14:2,3
Romans 1:16

15283724R00021

Made in the USA
Lexington, KY
19 May 2012